THE PLATE

The Who, What, Why, How, and How-Not-To's of Burn-Out

By Debbie Rhoads

KIDZMATTER
PUBLISHING

The Plate: The Who, What, Why, How, and How-Not-To's of Burn-Out

Published by KidzMatter
432 East Val Lane, Marion, IN 46952

Printed in the United States of America

Unless otherwise indicated, all Scripture quotations are taken from the Holy Bible, New Living Translation, copyright © 1996, 2004, 2015 by Tyndale House Foundation. Used by permission of Tyndale House Publishers, Carol Stream, Illinois 60188, USA. All rights reserved.

Scripture quotations taken from the Amplified® Bible (AMP), Copyright © 2015 by The Lockman Foundation. Used by permission. lockman.org

Cover design by Nicole Jones - kneecoalgrace@gmail.com
Interior layout by Nicole Jones - kneecoalgrace@gmail.com
Edited by Theda Crawford- thedacrawford4133@gmail.com

ISBN: 979-8-9850095-5-2
ISBN (ebook): 979-8-9850095-0-7

ENDORSEMENTS

In "The Plate," Debbie Rhoads delivers a vital and transformative guide for ministry leaders seeking to avoid burnout and maintain a balanced life. With profound insights and practical strategies, this book equips readers with the tools to navigate the challenges of leadership while safeguarding their well-being. Debbie will help readers stay on course, ensuring their ministries thrive without sacrificing personal health and happiness. A must-read for anyone in a leadership role, "The Plate" offers invaluable wisdom for enduring success in both ministry and life.

> Ryan Frank
> CEO & Publisher
> KidzMatter

The Plate is a practical read for every ministry leader, whether you're on the edge of burnout or trying to avoid unhealth and crisis, this reader-friendly book is a must for your ministry library. Debbie, herself, is one of the most capable leaders I've ever had the privilege to work with and her strength of leadership and earned wisdom shines through in every thought, illustration, and transparent example.

> Jessica Bealer
> Director of Ministry Engagement
> Generis

Debbie Rhoads gives us an incredible resource about walking through and overcoming burnout in a way that simply makes sense. She shares her heart as she presents relatable approaches to adjust the course, we're on and what we can do to "fix" what may be on our plates. You'll absolutely want to have this book handy for yourself and to be able to share it with others. The Plate is a must-read!

Mitch Jensen
Assistant Pastor
Church of the Heartland – Plymouth, IN

The Plate is a practical guide to understanding and avoiding "burn-out". Through the imagery of plates and great stories from life experience, Debbie illustrates how "burn-out" happens, and how to fix it. I highly recommend leaders to embrace the wisdom in Debbie's book.

B-SHOC
Music Evangelist

A delicious analogy! An insightful and vulnerable look at a topic too many of us try to ignore. Debbie has bravely dished out the honest wake-up call we all need to avoid the pitfalls of burnout.

Laura Ottaviano
Director
Giant Kids Ministry

Debbie is a seasoned and experienced leader which can only be said because of her faithfulness over the years to what God has called her to. I believe the authority and wisdom she shares with us is because of first-hand revelation. Come sit at the table and get ready for the feast she has prepared for us.

Yancy

Songwriter, Worship Leader & Author

Debbie shares her passion and experience in addressing a very personal challenge that all leaders face...burnout. The stories she shares are entertaining, relatable, and very real! The Plate is an easy place to start addressing this sometimes-difficult topic.

Kevin and Alicia Weiers

Creators

iTeachChurch

TO ROB

You believe in me even when I don't believe in myself.
Thank you.

TABLE OF CONTENTS

foreword

In a world that seems to spin faster with each passing day, we find ourselves relentlessly pushing the boundaries of achievement, driven by the pursuit of success, productivity, and fulfillment. We are continually bombarded with the pressure to excel in our efforts to reach children and families, while simultaneously maintaining vibrant social lives, and keeping up with the ever-evolving technological landscape. Yet, beneath this facade of progress lies a shadow that has crept into the lives of countless children's ministry leaders—a shadow known as burnout.

In her own whimsical way, Debbie Rhoads addresses this silent suffering by inviting all of us to examine just how much we have on our proverbial plates. As children's ministry leaders and workers, we can all too easily ignore how our seemingly unwavering commitment to the ministry can drain our energy, chip away at our motivation, and dim the spark that once ignited our ministry passions.

With this resource, Debbie sheds light on this pressing issue that has long been obscured in the shadows. Bringing to bear her impressive collection of insights, stories, and practical strategies born out of decades of children's ministry experience, Debbie effectively dismantles the stigma surrounding burnout and fosters a space for open dialogue and under-standing.

This book is not just about the problem—it is about solu-tions. You will explore a multitude of tools and coping mecha-nisms to help readers navigate the labyrinth of burnout. From organization and boundary-setting techniques to embracing fun and delegation strategies, she equips children's ministry leaders with the tools to combat burnout head-on.

As you embark on this journey through the pages of this book, I urge you to reflect on your own experiences and those of others around you. Burnout is a legitimate threat to those of called to minister to children and families, but by under-standing the complexities of burnout, we can more effectively ward against its devastating impacts on our children's minis-try departments.

While the path to recovery may be arduous, it is not insurmountable. You couldn't ask for a better navigator than Debbie Rhoads. I have personally witnessed the pro-found impact she has had on so many children, families, and those entrusted to serve them. She is a leader among lead-ers. Despite the heavy weight she bears as a mother, grand-mother, wife, and leader across several large churches, Debbie does so with a grace, humility, and zeal that has withstood the test of time.

Let us embark on this transformative journey together, for within these pages lies the power to rekindle the sacred flame of hope and perseverance that resides within each of us.

Are you ready to examine your plate?

Esther Moreno
Founder of Child's Heart LLC

Our Pastor and Executive Team held a one-day leadership retreat off-site for all the staff that directly report to them. There were 15 of us in the room, including myself. One of the main initiatives was creating a culture of self-awareness. This included being able to give and accept feedback…and doing something with the feedback, if necessary. This was not new to any of us. We had been working on this for the past couple of years. As a church leadership team, we embraced it because it was making our organization better.

On this day, we were doing an exercise to help us develop this culture. They had us all sit in a circle and we were told to have a notepad and pen. For each person, we were going to answer two questions: How does this person positively impact our church/ministry? What does this person need to improve on to be a better leader? It sounds simple enough. It was not as easy as it sounded.

Round one. A two-minute timer was set. Within the two minutes, we were to assess this person answering both questions. (Remember, we were going to do this for all 15 of us in the room.) After two minutes, the timer would go off. The person we were assessing had to go first with THEIR answer for themself. What is your greatest impact? They would answer and then we would go around the circle and read what each of us wrote down. It was actually really cool to encourage each other in this way by hearing what your peers thought of you. However, then it was time for the other question.

What do they need to improve on to be a better leader? Before I tell you the rest of this story, I must tell you that there was one rule we had to follow. We had to sit there and accept it and we could not offer up any sort of explanation. Once again, the person we were assessing went first on their own self-assessment of what THEY thought they needed to improve on. This was followed by going around and each of us reading what we wrote down while the other staff member sat there and accepted the feedback. We went around the circle round after round. This was not as difficult and scary as I originally thought it would be. Then it was my turn.

I sat up nice and tall and straight. I was ready to tackle anything they threw at me. Leadership development is my jam, and I was weirdly excited for this peer feedback…until it happened.

Question #1, How does this person positively impact our church/ministry? Pause. You would think it would be easy to sit there and hear all the staff leaders sing your praises. Nope, at least not for me. I couldn't wait for this part to end. I was squirming in my seat…bring on the areas of improvement.

Question #2, What does this person need to improve on as a leader? I sat back up tall and straight. I had my notebook and pen ready to go so I could write down all the things because 14 people were about to tell me how I can improve as a leader. They went around the circle and 12 out of the 14 people sitting with me said THE EXACT SAME THING!!!

Wait!!! What is going on??? This must be a conspiracy against me. This did not happen to the others in the room. Why is everyone ganging up on me?

Ok, here's the thing. When one person gives you feedback, you listen, you process, and you let it hang out in your head and maybe you consider if you need to do something about it. When two people give you the same feedback, you give it a little more thought. When three people give you the same feedback, you stop and think, ok, maybe I need to seriously consider this. However, when 12 out of 14 people give you the exact same feedback, you better take heed.

My peers collectively told me that to improve as a leader I was headed for burn out and that I needed to slow down. Seriously? They were sitting here telling me to work less??? The words were not exact for each person; however, the statements were things like, you work too many hours, you need to protect your boundaries, you need to actually take your days off, you need to slow down, you need to pace yourself, blah, blah, blah… However, the statement that knocked me upside the head was, "You think that you are hiding it, but I can see through you…you are overwhelmed and headed for burnout." OUCH.

Time out.

I was sitting in this circle processing these things. How is this bad? I'm killin' it! My ministry area is rockin'! I'm on top of my game right now and you are telling me to "slow down"? Well, if this isn't a glaring blind spot. The problem is, I know better. I painstakingly work to protect the staff and volunteers who report to me to ensure they do not burn out, yet here I am headed in that direction.

As my pastor, executive team, and other staff leaders share their feedback with me; I refrain from saying anything and just smile and write down all their words.... even though they are all the same. When they finished, I couldn't help but chuckle and say, "So, is it weird that I am currently writing a book about burnout?" Of course, everyone burst into laughter.

Last year, I was at a children's ministry conference where I heard author and speaker, Beth Guckenberger say, "If you are going to write, write something you wish you stumbled upon." Well, here it is. The book that I know God gave to me. The book that I trust will be used to help many assess and overcome the frustration of burnout...hopefully, before it happens. The book I intended to be completely for others... God meant for me, too.

I don't have to tell you that burnout is not fun. If you haven't personally experienced it, you know someone who has, or you have at least been dangerously close to it. Burnout will rob you of joy and of great blessings that God has for your life. Let's be honest, many times, burnout is self-inflicted. I'm not saying ALL the time. I know there are circumstances that may be beyond our control. However, we may be in a crazy life season and choose to keep all the things on our life plate. This will surely lead to burnout.

Throughout this book, we are going to talk about our "life-plate." What size is the plate we are carrying, what is on our plate, how it got there, who is eating from it, and so on. We are going to examine habits that get us into trouble, best practices for boundaries, and what to do when things get out of hand, and we are ready to just throw our plate on the floor.

We are not meant to live a life of burnout. So, let's dig into the who, what, why, how, and how not-to's of burnout.

"Then Jesus said, "Come to me, all of you who are weary and carry heavy burdens and I will give you rest. Take my yoke upon you. Let me teach you, because I am humble and gentle at heart, and you will find rest for your souls. For my yoke is easy to bear, and the burden I give you is light."
-Matthew 11:28-30

THE WHO, WHAT, AND WHY OF BURNOUT

Before we can get started, we need to get into the nitty-gritty of burnout. The word gets thrown around loosely, however when examined, the enormity of burnout is unsettling.

WHAT?

Merriam-Webster defines burnout as: "exhaustion of physical or emotional strength or motivation usually as a result of prolonged stress or frustration." Or the verb for burnout is: "to cause to fail, wear out, or become exhausted especially from overwork or overuse." On a small scale, we can be burnt out on something like pizza because we have eaten it so much in a short amount of time. Or, one can be burnt out in one specific area of their life. However, most of the time, when burnout happens, it affects all of you. For example, if you are burnt out on your job, chances are the effects will flow over to other areas of your life, as well. Burnout will affect you physically, emotionally, and spiritually (Merriam-Webster failed to recognize the spiritual part.)

Having stress and frustration in life is inevitable. We will also sometimes find ourselves exhausted and our strength waning. However, it is when we carry these things for long periods of time that burnout happens.

Burnout is real. We need to educate ourselves about it. What is it? What are the signs? Why does it happen? How can I know if it's happening to me? What do I do if I'm burnt out? Is there life after burnout? We will address all these questions because burnout:

...lies to you.

...sneaks up on you.

...makes you feel inadequate.

...is brutal.

...a family destroyer.

...a job destroyer.

...a life destroyer.

...has the ability to take you out of the ministry.

...is a weapon of the enemy.

...is avoidable.

...can be redeemed.

WHO?

Who is susceptible to burnout? EVERYONE! I have only met one person in all my years that has told me that they have never been burnt out. Of course, I questioned his claim greatly. However, he insists that he has always lived his life in a way that burnout has never happened. While I remain a bit skeptical, I am quite intrigued...and a little jealous.

The reality is all of us are prone to burnout at some point in our lives. While it is possible to avoid it, many, if not most of us fall prey to it. We expect to see burnout in a new mom who is up for days on end with a newborn baby. We expect to see burnout in a college student who has multiple classes and is working a job to get through school. There are seasons in life where burnout is expected, and we are not surprised by it, but we are surprised when we see burnout happen to those who give their time to God's ministry. How can we become burnt out doing God's work? Unfortunately, it happens...a lot.

Like I said everyone is susceptible to burnout, however, it is these who are the most:

...those who have their priorities out of order.

...those who have a hard time saying no.

...those who think they must do everything themselves.

...those who struggle to relinquish control.

...those who think nobody can do things as well as they can.

...those who want to do "all the things".

...those who have FOMO (fear of missing out).

...those who think they must be involved in everything.

...those who are not clear of the direction and are searching.

...those with no boundaries.

Do you relate?

WHY?

Let's break down why burnout happens. We can do this by looking at the list of who is the most susceptible. Having just one of these habits/traits can lead you to a life of burnout.

1. Messed up priorities. When our priorities get out of whack, it is not usually done on purpose. Most of the time it starts with good intentions. An example would be when one is working extra hours to earn money for a family vacation. The vacation money is achieved, however, sights are then set on other things, and then more things. Before you know it, work becomes the priority over the family. The person is now working too much and struggling to keep up with the family. They become overwhelmed, exhausted, and frustrated.

2. **Not being able to say no.** Those with a big heart and who love to do things for people can get themselves in a lot of trouble if they are not careful. The ability to say no is a wonderful trait to have and can save one from the burden of burnout. We all have people we know that if we call them for anything they will say yes. They are our "go to" people. Beware of burning out your "go to" people. You may be one of those "go to" persons for someone else. Beware of burnout.

3. **"I don't need any help. I can do it all by myself."** Have you ever said this? This is where we need to remember that God did not put us on earth to do life alone. The next two will help us understand why we say this…

4. **Being a control freak.** I admit, I like to be in control. I like things done a certain way. Who can relate? We don't allow others to help us because that means we must relinquish control. However, that control can cause great trouble and bring on the burnout.

5. **"Nobody can do things as well as me."** Yes, I have said this statement. I'm not proud of it, but I'm just being honest. It comes from that control we just talked about. The truth is, this is a self-centered and an unfair assumption that brings us to burnout quickly.

6. **All the things.** One of the awesome things about the world we live in now is the fact that we have options. There

are so many things to choose from. The things meant to make our lives simple have clogged it up. The vast internet, cell phones, computers, apps, social media, streaming channels, and more. There really is no such thing as simple anymore. These things leave us with the longing of wanting more. Wanting to be a part of more, doing more, having more, being more. This constant pressure is sure to lead to being overwhelmed and not being able to keep up.

7. **Fear of missing out.** This goes along with wanting to do all the things and be all the things. We think if we don't do something or stop doing something that we will miss out. This fear will lead us right into a life of exhaustion.

8. **Needing to be involved in all things.** This isn't the same as the fear of missing out. This is when we think so highly of ourselves that we need to be a part of everything to keep things running. We may not say this out loud. However, actions of not relinquishing duties to others, or not training others screams this loud and clear.

9. **Unclear direction in life.** Maybe you are finding yourself searching. You are unclear of the direction of your life; therefore, you decide to do all the things until you figure it out. Trying new things along your journey is not a bad thing; however, remember, that you do not have to do them all at the same time.

10. **No boundaries = burnout.** I used to joke about boundaries. I would say, "What are these boundaries you speak of?" I didn't see the need. I felt that as a person in ministry I needed to make myself available all the time to all the people. Whew! I was wrong! Boundaries protect us from burnout!

Now that we have more of an understanding of the who, what, and why of burnout, let's dig in to see what is on our plate.

Keeping it Real:

In what area(s) do you see yourself most susceptible when it comes to burnout?

How does burnout make you feel?

What kind of boundaries do you have to protect yourself from burnout?

HOW BIG IS YOUR PLATE?
Your season of life will determine your plate size

My husband and I were at the cocktail hour of a wedding. In the middle of the room there was a beautiful display of appetizers. The bride and groom made sure there was something for every taste and dietary restriction. It was overwhelming…and quite fantastic. We walked up to partake of the awesomeness, and we started by picking up a plate. My husband held the plate up and said, "Really? They expect me to eat off such a tiny plate?" Embarrassed, I hushed my husband and tried to explain to him that this was just the cocktail hour. We are not supposed to eat a lot right now because soon we will sit down for the main meal. If they give you a small plate, they only want you to eat a little bit. My answer did not satisfy him. He proceeded to pick up TWO plates and load them up with all the delicious appetizers. Now when I say he loaded them up, I mean he LOADED THEM UP! He partook of all the things, and he ate everything on his plate…I mean PLATES.

Fast-forward about 45 minutes later, the doors of the reception hall opened and we went in and found our seats where we were then served a lavish and quite-hearty meal.

My husband looked down at his plate of food that was just put before him and said, "Do you think they have take-home boxes? I can't eat this. I'm full." I didn't have to say anything, my smirk screamed, "I told you so!"

Let's talk about the size of your plate. I'm going to call it your "life-plate." It's the plate you are given to add things to. The things you are responsible for. The things you choose to do in your life. Yes, you get to choose what is put onto your plate. (We will talk about this more in future chapters.)

There are times we use the wrong size plate for our season of life. Plates are not one size fits all and neither are our seasons of life. What you can take on and accomplish in one season of life will definitely be different in another. We may say we don't need a smaller plate; we just won't fill up the plate we have. That concept sounds good; however, we live in a world that is fast-paced and with pressures to do all the things, be all things, all the time. It's when we fall into this trap that burnout comes.

> *Dinner Plate*
> *[din-uhr pleyt]*
> *noun*
> *1. the standard, basic capacity holder of our lives.*

The "Dinner Plate" is the basic plate. This is the plate that is the "normal" plate with a normal workflow in life. We use the dinner plate for our main meals because it has a larger capacity.

When we are young, our life-plate usually has lots of extra room on it. We have time for extracurricular activities.

As we grow older, we add things like college, career, ministry, marriage, and kids. We begin to add things like homework with the kids, PTO, kids' sports, kids' music lessons, life groups at church, working out, or volunteering. We can't forget family time, friendships, and continued date nights with the spouse, oh, and hopefully a vacation every now and then. Then there are household chores, yard work to keep the HOA off your back, upkeep on your vehicle, grocery shopping, and laundry. Let's make sure we don't leave out the most important thing on our plate...our relationship with God.

Dessert Plate
[di-zert pleyt]
noun
1. a smaller capacity holder, purposely meant to hold a limited amount.
2. normally holds just the sweet things in life.

There are seasons in life when we just do not have the capacity to hold all the things. It is during these times we are to purposely limit what is on our plate. Reality doesn't always make this easy.

Sometimes dessert plates are just too small. There is a buffet restaurant at one of our favorite vacation spots that we like to visit. Not only do they have a salad buffet and a main meal buffet, but they also have a dessert buffet. This dessert buffet is incredible! It has every kind of sweet treat you can imagine. However, they only give you a small dessert plate to make your selections. That seems so cruel and unfair. Then I got a great idea. I will get a dinner plate from the main buffet line and use it at the dessert bar. Brilliant!

May I remind you, I had already partaken from the salad buffet. I also already ate from the main meal buffet. However, those desserts…how could I only select what would fit on this tiny dessert plate? Wait, I know what you are thinking, if it's a smaller plate they want you to eat less. Isn't this what you told your husband at the wedding? Yes, but that doesn't matter in this situation…those desserts! I want them ALL! To my defense, I just wanted a small portion of each one.

I proceeded to add all the desserts onto my DINNER plate. I went back to the table to enjoy the deliciousness. As I ate my desserts, I began to not feel very well. But they are desserts…they are wonderful…I must have them. So, I pushed through my yucky feelings and continued to eat my dinner-sized dessert. By the end, I was just sick…literally. I left the restaurant feeling absolutely horrible. That evening, we had tickets to a show that I had been very much looking forward to. However, I missed most of it because I spent a good portion of my evening in the bathroom, miserable from my choice to eat too much from the wrong-sized plate. To make matters worse, it took me two days to feel better from my dessert debacle. I ruined part of my vacation.

Sometimes your life-plate HAS to be a dessert-sized plate. Sometimes we are not meant to have all the things on our plates or to even carry a regular-sized plate. However, we look around at life and say, "I must have that on my plate!" So, we put it on our plate, KNOWING that we shouldn't… but we do it anyway. We push through the feelings of being overwhelmed by bad choices until we end up sick…mentally, emotionally, physically and spiritually sick. There are times when you have to give yourself permission to live off of a smaller plate. I feel like I have to repeat that last statement… give yourself permission to live off of a smaller plate.

What do I mean by this, and what constitutes life on a dessert-sized plate? There are seasons in life when we must slow down and allow God to give us a smaller plate for a while. This doesn't mean you will always have to live life off of the small dessert plate. It means, you just need some time to breathe and maybe just focus on fewer things. After all, if you are given a small plate, you are meant to have less on your plate. Sometimes that focus is just the sweeter things in life.

At the age of 30, I was diagnosed with stage 3 breast cancer. My kids were young…I was young. I was determined to keep life as normal as possible. I decided that nothing in life would change. In my mind, I was going to keep up with my same work schedule, kid's sports schedules, all the things, all the time. It's just a couple surgeries and chemo and radiation, no big deal, right? God was handing me a smaller plate and I pushed it away and kept my dinner plate. It was too heavy for me. I was physically, emotionally, mentally, and spiritually weak. I floundered. I was overwhelmed, exhausted, and felt like a failure most of the time.

This makes me think of my grandson who loves to do things by himself. However, he's three years old and still requires help for some things, whether he agrees with that or not. It was Pops' birthday and he wanted to carry the plate with the birthday cake on it. He said, "I do it, Gigi. I don't need help." I hesitantly handed him the plate telling him to use two hands. He was all smiles as he proudly carried that plate across the room to Pops. I walked beside him with my hands right next to the plate ready to catch it if/when it began to fall to the floor. Luckily, the cake safely made it to Pops and the carpet remained intact and unstained. However, that was quite a stressful transaction for Gigi. There was a moment the cake was literally sideways. I don't even know how it stayed on the plate.

That was me at age 30, bald from chemo, holding my big ol' dinner life-plate with two hands trying to do it all by myself. After a while, I did finally realize I was being unreasonable in that season of my life and took hold of the dessert plate. Life was much more manageable and enjoyable. However, it was not before I experienced tons of unnecessary stress, tears, and frustration.

You may be feeling God trying to hand you a smaller life-plate right now.

- You are having marriage problems and you know you need to slow down and deal with it, but all the things….
- Your health is really not good. You have neglected yourself for years. You have felt for a long time that you need to slow down and get a handle on it, but all the things…
- Your child is struggling. He/she is struggling in school. He/she is struggling socially. He/she really needs your attention, but all the things…
- Your church has been going through a church split and you have been dealing with all aspects of it

for a couple of years. You are spiritually and emotionally spent, but all the things….

You know if God is speaking to you. You know if you can handle what is currently on your plate in your current season in life. Sometimes no change is necessary, but sometimes it is. Don't ignore it, my friend. It may be God trying to get you to focus on just a few things in this season.

I will take a moment and talk about the flip side. Yes, I am very much aware that there are people who live off of a smaller dessert plate and should be on a dinner plate. Maybe at one time they were in a season of a small plate, but have stayed there and not ventured back out to do more in life. Or, they choose to use it as an excuse to not take on more in life. If you are reading this book about burnout, this is most likely not you. As frustrating and irritating as it may be to watch people make excuses and not do more in life, we will allow God to deal with them. This book is about you.

Platter
[pla-ter]
noun
1. an extra-large capacity holder for special seasons in life, only meant to be used occasionally.

The platter is only meant for special occasions. I have one really big platter and I only use it for parties and during the holidays. Other than these times, I rarely use it. This doesn't mean I don't need it. I am very grateful to have it when it's time to put out the Thanksgiving turkey or I am trying to create a fun party spread. It is not meant to be used all the time.

From time to time, our life-plate will be a platter. For example, as a Children's Ministry Director, Vacation Bible School is a platter season. It's a time when there is a lot of extra on my plate. It's a lot to handle and a lot to deal with, however, it's just for a short season and then the platter gets put away.

I highly recommend that you plan out when your platter seasons are. Ensure they are not too close to each other and limit the length of these seasons. We are definitely not meant to carry around platters as our life-plate for the long term.

Keeping it Real:

How close to burnout do you feel right now?

What size life-plate are you currently holding?

Are you freaked out by the thought of taking on a smaller plate? Why?

Have you ever felt you should have been living from a dessert plate, but you held onto your dinner plate? What affect did it have in your life?

Are you currently working from a platter? How long have you been in this season? What is it going to take for you to put the platter away?

MY EYES ARE BIGGER THAN MY STOMACH
Not being able to say no to adding things to your plate

"Your eyes are bigger than your stomach." That has always been a strange phrase to me. My mom used to say it when we scooped too much food onto plates at mealtime. My mom would make a delicious meal and if you wanted it, you better put it on your plate the first time, because I guarantee you there would not be any more left after all 7 kids got theirs. This phrase was generally said to my brother who was the youngest. He learned the hard way that if he didn't take it, he wasn't going to get it. However, once he had it on his plate, he had to deal with it. That was the problem. He would always take more than he could handle.

Does this sound familiar? Have you ever taken on more than you can handle? When you added it to your life-plate, you thought it was a good idea. It looked like something you wanted, something you needed, and something you had to have on your plate. Then you looked at your plate and realized that your "eyes were bigger than your stomach." This leads to what I like to call self-inflicted burnout.

One of the big causes of self-inflicted burnout is our FOMO (fear of missing out).

Why do we do that to ourselves? Do we really feel like we have to be a part of all things? All the time? I am going to be honest and answer, yes. I do like to be a part of everything. I don't like to miss out on things. FOMO is real. FOMO also gets us into trouble because it causes us to fill up our plates with unnecessary things.

Our society says to do all the things. You can do it all, you can be it all, and you can have it all. Reality says, sure, but all the stress and burnout comes along with that. When you choose to be okay with not being a part of everything and allowing something to NOT be on your plate, you make room for rest and peace of mind, and for God to move. How can God move in your life if your plate is so full there is nowhere to go? I don't like to miss out, but I have learned that having room for God to move is so much better. He usually ends up giving me things I would never have imagined because I stopped chasing all the other things. I would rather miss out on what the world has to offer and not miss out on what God has for me. THAT is where our FOMO should reside.

Another cause of self-inflicted burnout is having the mindset of, "I've always done this, so I have to keep doing it." My friend, I am here to tell you that you can stop doing things. Just because you have always done it, doesn't mean you have to always do it.

The worst cause of self-inflicted burnout is our inability to say no. It's hard to say no when someone asks you to do something. Especially if it's something we enjoy, if it's for a good cause, or if it's for a good friend. How could something good be bad for me, right? It won't take long. It's just one small thing. The next thing you know, your plate is so full of these little, small, good things that you are overwhelmed.

Here is what it comes down to:

- You do not have to be a part of everything.
- Just because you have always done something, doesn't mean you should keep doing it.
- It's ok to say no...even to things that are good. Just because it's good doesn't mean you should do it.

In his book, *Replenish*, Larry Witt talks about the seduction of ambition. Ambition, even godly ambition, can seduce us to do more, to be more.[1] There is nothing wrong with being ambitious; it's a good thing. However, when our ambition fills our life-plate to the point we can barely hold it, it leads to burnout.

Before you add something to your life-plate, ask yourself the following questions:

- Why am I adding this to my plate?
- Is there room on my plate, or am I just piling it on and HOPING I will be able to have the capacity to do it?
- Will this added thing bring me stress or joy? Let's be real, sometimes we have to do things that don't bring us joy...that's life.
- Is this added thing really necessary?

There are times in life you just have to say "no." No is not a bad word. It can actually be freeing. You should try it.

---

1. Witt, L. (2011). Replenish (1st ed., pp. 39-42). Baker Books.

Keeping it Real:

What have you said yes to recently that you wish you wouldn't have?

Have you fallen into the "I've always done this, so I have to keep doing it" trap?

What do you know you "should" take off of your plate, but you don't want to because of FOMO?

Make a list of things you would like to take off of your plate?

WHAT'S ON YOUR PLATE?
Organizing your stuff

Normally, if you look at a dinner plate, you can easily glance at the plate and be able to see all the contents. You can see each item. Some items take up more space than others, but you can see what is there. Then there are those days when you have a church potluck or a big family holiday dinner. There are tons of wonderful food to choose from and you add more and more to your plate. You feel the pressure to try Aunt Mary's jello salad; so even though your plate is full, you add that as well. The next thing you know the plate is piled up and you can't tell where one item starts and another ends. (Side note: For those of us freaking out right now about our food touching, just wait, a chapter for you is coming.)

Does your life-plate feel like this? Do you even know what is on your plate?

Or is there so much on your life-plate that you can't even tell anymore? You think you have a grasp on things, but then you lift up the meatloaf to find more mashed potatoes. Then you are like, "I thought I already ate all the mashed potatoes, now I have more to deal with." Despite this strange food/plate analogy, there is so much truth to this in real life. We see all the wonderful options that life has to offer, and we want to be a part of it. We add it to our life-plate. Now more than ever, in our society, there is much pressure to do everything. We say yes because it's just "one more thing". Opportunities come up. Job expectations increase. Our family grows. We take on more and more. There is nothing wrong with that. However, when we take on so much that we can't even tell what is clearly on our plate, we now have a problem. Burnout is on the horizon.

Now the question is, what do we do with an overloaded plate? Now that it's full, where do you go from here? Let's unpack the plate….

1. I need you to remember that your life-plate is YOURS to add to and YOURS to remove things from. I know, it's not that simple, but it's a fact.

2. This is not going to be an overnight fix. This will take time, however, it's so worth it.

3. It's going to take discipline. Chances are if you are in a season of a full life-plate, this is not the first time you have been here. If I had to guess, I would say that it's a pattern that rears its ugly head often. I may or may not be speaking from experience.

4. Before you can do anything, you must know what is actually on your life-plate. Schedule some time to sit down and start listing it out. You need to list out ALL THE THINGS! This is going to be tedious and daunting. Don't give up. It works and it's worth it. If anything, it's extremely eye-opening. This exercise may even take a couple of days or

even a week as you track all that you do. My suggestion is to break it down by categories: Home, Kids, Ministry, Work, Church, Etc. Then break it down even further. (Under work I have a, b, and c on my plate.) Then break it down even further still. (At work under a, I have x, y, and z.)

5. Examine your life-plate list. What does it show you? Where do you spend most of your time? What surprises you most about your list?

6. Now take it to God in prayer. "God, here is my life-plate. I am overwhelmed. I need wisdom on how to organize my life-plate and determine what should be on it. What should I keep? What should I take off? How can my life-plate bring honor to you and not lead me to burnout?"

7. Give yourself time to hear from God. Allow Him to work in your heart. There may be things on your life-plate that you are not willing to give up, but God is telling you to let go. Or God may want you to keep all the things on your plate, however, He is asking you to reorganize and restructure your schedule and how you do things.

Keeping it Real:

Do you have a hard time saying "no" to people when it comes to taking on more things?

Are you nervous about listing out what is on your life-plate? Why or why not?

How many times have you found yourself in burnout or close to burnout?

I DON'T WANT MY FOOD TO TOUCH
Boundaries

My grandma was a wonderful cook. It was common for all our family and friends to go to Grandma's house and have a meal. It didn't have to be a special occasion. We would all show up and she would feed us. It was her passion. Some of my favorite memories are of these times. However, I specifically remember one night that turns my stomach, still to this day.

This specific evening there seemed to be more people than usual. Grandma pulled out all the plates she had. Every plate, big and small. These were the days when paper plates were rare. We used "real" plates back in the day. I remember us talking about it, because the conversation was around who was going to do the dishes. As we were eating, my Uncle Gary showed up to join us. My young child's mind was very curious as to what he would do. There were no plates. How was he going to eat? Uncle Gary was completely unphased by this. He went to the cupboard and grabbed a bowl. Not just any bowl, a mixing bowl. He proceeded to add all his food into the bowl...meatloaf, creamed corn, mashed potatoes, gravy, and more. I was horrified. I cried, "Uncle Gary, your food is touching!"

To which he responded. "It all goes to the same place anyway." And he proceeded to MIX his food! Ahhhhhhhh!

Yes, I am one of those people who does not like my food to touch. I don't think it should be that way. The plate is big enough to keep them separate. If you can eat off of a plate with compartments, that's even better. Once food is intermingled together, it's ruined and is no longer edible.

I personally believe that it's important that a life-plate should have compartments. These compartments are boundaries that keep things from becoming intermingled. There is the family compartment, the ministry compartment, kids' sports compartment, etc., etc.

I am in a new season of life that I am learning to navigate. My kids are grown. I am in full-time ministry and my husband works a lot of hours at his job. With these changes in our lives, I realized that I began to open the compartments and allow things on my life-plate to run together. To be completely honest, I was ok with it. Ministry and home were all intermingled and I didn't see an issue. My husband didn't seem to have an issue with it either because of how much he was working. Then my husband began to realize that ministry was taking more of a precedence. There were no boundaries…at all. I was taking phone calls on my days off. I was at a point where I wasn't even taking days off. The idea of a Sabbath…nope, that wasn't happening either. I allowed ministry to take over so much that it was now affecting my home life, my health, and my relationships. I feel it needs to be said, the expectation of working so much was my own expectation.

It was not put on me by anyone. It was me being seduced by ambition.

Of course, I didn't mean for any of this to happen. Ministry is good, right? I mean, I am serving God and teaching kids about Jesus. How could this be bad? God wants me to serve Him, however, sacrificing my family and health are not a way to honor Him. I needed boundaries, badly. I will admit, I still struggle with boundaries. I am a work in progress. I am blessed to have a pastor and staff that set a culture of leading from a healthy place and they give room to be able to do that.

Now, let's go back to the story at the beginning of the book when the 12 out of 14 peers told me to slow down because I'm headed to burnout. Like I said, I know better. I work hard to ensure my team is healthy, yet here I was unhealthy. It was an example of "put the oxygen mask on yourself first."

After that staff exercise at the leadership retreat, we had a week to process the feedback we were given. Our instructions were to select one piece of feedback given and put together a plan of how you will implement it to become a better leader. Gee, I wonder what feedback I should choose. I had to get back to the basics of boundaries. Below you will find my plan. I am happy to tell you that I have worked the plan, and it works. I will also tell you, it is very easy to fall backward, so being determined to not go backward is crucial.

1. I looked at the calendar and scheduled some time off. I had banked up several comp days and hadn't used any vacation days for the year yet. Also, I am notorious for not using my vacation time and losing it. I scheduled days off that I could take within the next 3 months. I didn't look

at the whole year. I wasn't ready for that. One step at a time.

2. I created an "out of office" response for my email. Normally, this would only be used if I were on vacation. However, this was now going to be used on my days off. I find that it's really helpful to not feel pressure to respond to emails because they have seen that I am off.

3. I got people to hold me accountable. This was the hardest for me. Among those to hold me account- able is my kid's ministry staff. I am blessed to have the most incredible staff to work with. I really felt God nudging me to apologize to them for not setting a good example. My ambition and lack of boundaries was inadvertently putting pressure on them to do more. So, now THEY hold me accountable too.

4. My husband and I began putting our phones in a designated spot when we're trying to spend time together. This way we can be fully present and not have any interruptions.

Having compartments on our "life-plate" is a must. Of course, this is especially true if you are in a season where you are raising your children. Children learn by watching us. That is how they learn life boundaries.

Keeping it Real:

Do you like your food to touch?

How are your boundaries? Do you have any?

Do you regularly have a day for Sabbath? Why or why not?

Do you have any vacation days or time off scheduled?

GET A CLEAN PLATE
Can I get a clean "life-plate"?

One job I would not like to have is being the dishwasher at a buffet restaurant. There are so many dirty plates! They require you to get a clean plate every single time you go back up to the buffet. While I am grateful for this concept when it comes to germs, cross-contamination, and not having my new food touch any remnants of the other food that was on my plate; I can't help but think of all those dirty plates. Whew! It makes me want to tip the dishwasher.

Let's go back to your life-plate list that you created. You have been examining the list, and you have been praying to God about what should be on your plate. Can you start with a clean life-plate? The answer is yes. Sometimes we need to just get a new plate.

You have your new life-plate and now you have to decide, what goes back on the plate? Like I said before, YOU are the one who chooses what gets added to your life-plate and what gets removed from it. As you are working through the process of deciding what goes back on the plate, keep these things in mind:

- Your priorities may not match the priorities of someone else and that is ok. Don't give in to the pressure of matching the life-plate of someone else.
- You also get to decide how much space each thing will take up on the life-plate.
- Just because something has been on your life-plate for a really long time doesn't mean it has to stay on your life-plate. Seasons change.
- Consider your season of life.
- Normally, when you put something on a plate, you start with the main dish and then you add the side dishes. Start with the big stuff first.

Ok, here we go! Are you ready? Let's start deciding what gets put back on the life-plate. I want to remind you that this is not an easy process. It can actually be quite painful. However, it's a lot less painful and traumatic than burnout.

1. The main dish. I like to call these the non-negotiables. These are things that HAVE to be on your plate. Example: Your relationship with God, your spouse, your children, your job/ministry, school, your health, etc.

   - Don't wait until the end to make room for your relationship with God.
   - It is too simple to neglect our spouse. It's non-negotiable. Date your spouse!
   - Your kids. They need you…now. Please know that I am in no way insinuating that you cannot work or have a ministry while you are raising your kids. But I am

saying, having boundaries to ensure they don't get lost under the meatloaf are crucial.

- Your job/ministry. Of course, you need to work to survive. However, sometimes we need to evaluate if we are in the right place or if we need to make any adjustments in how much we are working.

2. The carb. The carb (rice or potatoes) of the meal is not the main dish, however, it is substantial on how it fills you up. These are the things you don't HAVE to do but are still really important. Example: Serving at church, being in a life group, friendships, etc.

    - We are not meant to do life alone. Therefore, being in a life group and taking time to foster friendships is vital.
    - We are called to be a part of the church, not to be consumers of a church.

3. The Vegetable. This is a healthy part of the life-plate. However, I also see this as things that you need to have on your plate that you may be able to get done with a "supplement." Example- housework, yardwork, upkeep on the car, laundry, etc. When I say supplement, I mean that maybe you are in a season where you can afford to hire a cleaning service to come once a month to help keep things going. Or, maybe you could pay the neighbor boy to cut your lawn, etc.

4. The Side Salad. This represents all the extra

things. Example- kids' sports, music lessons, dance classes, etc.

5. The Dessert. I like to refer to the dessert as all the fun stuff we put on our plates. Example: Vacation, fun activities, or simply just chilling out and watching TV.

May I reiterate that this can be a difficult process. The pressure is real as you do the work to determine your priorities. Keep in mind your end goal…to be healthy in your mind, body, and soul so you avoid burnout. I also want to remind you that this is just a basic guideline to get you started. Everybody's life-plate is unique and needs to be treated as such.

A word of advice to you if you end up feeling led to not put certain things back onto your life-plate. I highly recommend that you "quit/leave" something with a notice. Example, if you are coaching a kid's team, do not just say, "Peace, out! This doesn't fit on my plate anymore." Talk to whoever is in charge and give adequate notice so you leave on good terms and bridges are not burned. This may mean finishing up the season and not signing up for another. After all, this may be something you can add back onto your life-plate at another time.

Keeping it Real:

Are you freaking out?

Does this process give you hope?

YOU ARE NOT LEAVING THE TABLE UNTIL YOU EAT EVERYTHING ON YOUR PLATE
Mastering the Art of Delegation

My mom was a stickler for us to eat everything on our plates. After all, there are starving children in Africa. While that was true and still is to this day, I still never understood that concept. If they were starving, why couldn't I just send the food I am not eating to Africa. It would be a win-win for everyone. I didn't realize it then, but I already had a mindset for delegation.

I hate peas. I have always hated peas. I was told that as I got older, I would learn to like them. Nope. As I got older, I was old enough to decide to get my vegetable nutrients from vegetables that I actually liked. Anyway, one night my mom made peas to go with our dinner. I can still smell them. Eww. As a child, I had a trick where if there was something I didn't like to eat, I would take a bite and then have a drink of water or a bite of the other food on my plate right after to help the taste go away. However, that didn't work with peas. I just couldn't stomach them. This particular night, I managed to get a couple peas down. It was brutal. I ate everything else on my plate, but I left the peas. It was at this moment I really wished we had a dog. My mom told me that I could not leave the table until I ate my peas. Well, I decided it was going to be a long night.

I sat at that table until bedtime. No peas eaten. I was basically paralyzed. I simply just couldn't do it and because of this, nothing else on my child life-plate could be done. No playing with my Barbie dolls, and no making food that didn't contain peas in my Easy Bake Oven.

Frustrated, my mom sent me to bed with the promise that these peas would be waiting for me at breakfast.

Well, when my mom made a promise, you could count on her following through. Peas for breakfast. Brutal. Just brutal. Please God, how can I send these peas to Africa? Then again, I didn't think they would even eat the peas. The morning passed. The peas sat there as I sang to myself and created stories in my head.

Lunch time came. You guessed it, peas!!! So brutal.

Pause. Don't go judging my mom. She was not starving me. No one was harmed in this attempt to get me to eat peas.

By about 2pm, my mom gave up. That was a "God" moment for me. "Well, I guess you don't like peas." What gave you that idea?

My mom made me a bologna sandwich and sent me outside to play with my sister. My number 2 food that I hate right next to peas is bologna. Thank God, she sent me outside, so I was able to delegate the eating of the bologna to my sister. I ate the bread and she ate the nasty bologna.

Why did I tell you this story? To get my point across that delegation is a great way to get things on your life-plate.

To be honest, as an adult it did take me a bit to fully embrace the concept of delegation. I would make all the excuses:

- I like things done a certain way.
- It's easier to just do it myself.
- I don't have time to train anyone.
- Nobody can do it as well as I do.
- What if they do it better than me? (Just keeping it real….)

It wasn't until I had been in full-time ministry for several years before I realized it's the only way I am going to grow as a leader, as a person, and to be able to increase the capacity of my life-plate. I even implemented this at home.

When my boys were younger, I was that mom that thought I had to take care of everything myself. They did some chores, but I only had them do certain things. I did most of the household chores. Hindsight, not a good idea. Anyway, it was a week before my oldest son was leaving for college when we realized he had no idea how to do laundry. He was 18 years old. What have I done? I have completely failed as a mom. That entire week we were washing everything in the house to give him practice so I felt better about sending him off into the world knowing how to do his own laundry. To my defense, in the back of my mind I just expected him to bring his laundry home on the weekends. Isn't that what all college kids do? Then I realized, his college was a bit further away and coming home every weekend wasn't doable.

During that week, I decided that my younger son who is 5 years younger needed to learn this life skill. So, from that moment on, I delegated his laundry to him, and I never did a stitch of his laundry after that.

Most of my delegation skills have been mastered within my ministry. At first, it was difficult and not fun. However, as I leaned into the concept, I began to see the benefits of delegation:

- It increases your capacity.
- It gives ownership to those you delegate to.
- You develop leadership skills in others, as you give them the opportunity to learn new things.
- God elevates you, as you lift others up.
- You get a lot more stuff done!

Delegation works within your ministry, your job, and your home, etc. As you are deciding what gets placed back on your life-plate, consider delegation as a way to restructure how you do things. I could actually write an entire book about how to delegate, but here are a few easy steps to get you started:

1. Take out your exhaustive life-plate list that you made. Ask yourself the question, "What are things that only I can do?" I didn't say what things you WANT to do, however, things that only YOU can do. Yes, there may be some training involved. That comes later. For now, just focus on things only you can do.

2. Now, you should be left with things you can delegate. Start considering, to whom can you delegate things? This does take some thinking. You don't want to delegate some tasks to just anyone. Look for hidden talents and abilities.

3. Have the needed conversation with them. Example, when I delegated writing preschool curriculum, I explained why I think she would do well in that area. I then took the time to give my expectations and trained her.
4. Remember, if you do not give clear expectations, you will not get what you expect. They can't read your mind.
5. Follow up. Check in and see how it's going. I like to say, trust, but verify.
6. Don't take it back! Be careful not to fall into the trap of going back to "help" and taking the task back. You are defeating the purpose.
7. Show appreciation and give feedback in a timely manner.
8. If you give a task to someone and they really mess up or drop the ball, don't give up. Use it as a learning experience and keep leaning in.
9. Remember, delegation is NOT bossing people around and just giving your workload away. It's meant to increase your capacity and elevate others.

If you are not well-versed in the art of delegation, hold on! You are going to love it! Don't quit! It takes some time to master it. It's worth it!

Keeping it Real:

How would you rate your delegation skills?

What is the main reason you choose not to delegate?

HOW DID THIS GET ON MY PLATE?
When YOUR plate spills over onto someone else's plate

Somewhere along the way, I got the idea in my head that overfilling my life-plate only affected me. After all, I am not asking anyone else to do the things on my plate. I am the one taking on the responsibility, not them. I was wrong.

As I was continually striving to be self-aware, I realized that my ambition was taking a toll on my assistant. Now, I have the best assistant EVER! She is a rockstar and I couldn't do what I do without her. Last year, I took on a couple "side ministries" that I didn't think would affect anyone. I knew that my life-plate was already full, however, that whole ambition thing....

At first it seemed like all was well, then I started noticing that she seemed a little stressed and I couldn't figure out why. I was checking in on her about how she was doing personally? How was her family? Etc.? However, I didn't ask her about her workload because in my mind, nothing had changed for her. I was the one with an increased workload, not her.

What I didn't see was that because my workload increased, I was slower at getting things to my assistant that she required to do her job...and she has a system. I was throwing a big kink in it. Because of the amazing person that she is and her dedication to helping me, she began seeing where I needed help and took the initiative to pick up my slack. After a while, it began to wear her down. She did not have room for this on her life-plate, nor did she give permission for or even want me to add this to her. My choice to overfill my plate spilled over onto hers. That was a tough realization and lesson learned.

Whether we like it or not, our life-plate choices affect everyone around us. These "side ministries" also inadvertently affected things at home, as well. I was more tired which made me grumpy and irritable. I also got behind in my housework, which made me even more grumpy and irritable. My poor husband. So, while I was the one who technically took on these "side ministries," those closest to me suffered.

Keeping it Real:

Have you ever taken on something and noticed that it affected those around you?

What are you like when you are over-extended?

CHUCKING YOUR PLATE IN THE FLOOR
When You Are Overwhelmed and Just Done

One of the few good things that happened in 2020 is that I became a Gigi. Let me tell you, having grandkids is the best thing EVER! It's like God saying, "Well, done thou good and faithful servant while you are still here on Earth." When my son and his wife had their first child, they were 26 years old. So, it had been 26 years since I was fully submerged into the life of a newborn. Yes, I am a children's ministry director and I strive to stay relevant on all things kids; however, I wasn't aware of some of the cool new inventions and gadgets they now have for infants/toddlers. As my grandson became old enough to start eating solid food, they would put him in a highchair with a little plate and he would eat from that plate (with compartments, of course). It was adorable. However, when my sweet adorable, precious grandson, who could do no wrong in my eyes, was done eating...he was done! He was ready to just get out of his chair. He wanted the plate removed and he wanted to get down. If his wishes were not granted fast enough, he would pick up his plate and chuck it onto the floor.

The next time I came over, I saw that the plate they gave my adorable, precious grandson looked a little different. This one had a big suction cup on the bottom that stuck to the table. When my sweet boy was done and attempted to chuck that plate onto the floor, that plate remained securely attached to the table. Such a brilliant invention!

I was there - right where my sweet, adorable grandson was. I had been "eating from my life-plate," but I was done. I had enough and I wanted the plate to be taken away. Please someone take this from me and just let me get out of this restraint of pressure that is holding onto me and let me be free from all my responsibilities. If I don't get relief, I am just going to chuck this plate in the floor and I do not care about the consequences. Can anyone relate?

I know that sometimes I joke about burnout, or I will make light of it; however, it is no laughing matter. It is downright dangerous. Burnout can:

- Take away your health.
- Rob you of your joy.
- Skew your perspective.
- Cause undue stress.
- Affect your relationships.
- Be passed on to your family…even your kids.
- Take you out of the ministry and what God called you to do.
- Affect your job.
- Affect your attitude.
- Give you anxiety.
- Ruin your life.

Matthew 11:28-30 has become my absolutely favorite go-to scripture when I feel like chucking my plate. Let me show you how God interpreted it for me:

Jesus said,
Hey, come here, I'm here for you. I haven't left you; I've been here the whole time waiting.
Hand me that plate, it looks really heavy and it looks like you are struggling.
I've got you. This isn't heavy for me at all.
Why don't you just rest for a bit and catch your breath.
Let me show you how to manage this better.
I'm not judging you or beating you down.
I just want to help you find rest for your soul.
My way makes life a lot easier.

"Then Jesus said, "Come to me, all of you who are weary and carry heavy burdens and I will give you rest. Take my yoke upon you. Let me teach you, because I am humble and gentle at heart, and you will find rest for your souls. For my yoke is easy to bear, and the burden I give you is light."
Matthew 11:28-30

Keeping it Real:

Have you ever wanted to just chuck your life-plate onto the floor?

What stopped you?

What is God saying to you right now?

EVERYTHING ON MY PLATE IS THE SAME COLOR
Adding Fun to Your Life

I didn't take much interest in cooking until I was married, and then I had to. The summer before my senior year of high school, my mom had to have a surgery that put her out of commission for about a month while she healed. As the oldest child, she depended on me to help take care of my siblings by grocery shopping and cooking for them.

My siblings never really complained much, they were fine with my simple meals, most of the time. One night, I made a meal that consisted of fish sticks, Kraft macaroni and cheese, and corn. I was pretty proud of myself. My sister looked down at the plate and said, "Everything is the same color."

To which I replied, "Who cares what color it is, it's all good to eat."

She responded with, "There is supposed to be a pop of color on the plate."

What??? First of all, you are a kid. What do you know about "a pop of color on the plate?" Does that really matter?

Just so you know, it has been decades since that conversation and every time I make a meal, I make sure that there is a "pop of color" on the plate.

Sometimes in life we need a pop of color. We get stuck on the details of our life-plate and just doing the same things over and over and over again. We don't take any time for fun. Last year, I was asked what my hobbies were. What do you do for fun? It was very sobering that I didn't have an answer. I have allowed myself to be so bogged down that I no longer have hobbies. I used to….a really long time ago. Back in the day. What do I do for fun? All I could think of is that when I do have down time, I usually just veg out on the couch watching Netflix. That's not really fun, it's more numbing than anything.

This has sent me on a quest to discover fun. I have been trying to learn what I like to do. Do I even like the hobbies I used to like? What is fun for me now? I have had to really search because I found that fun was taking me away from life-plate plans and I was becoming frustrated by it. This part of my journey has been forcing me to ensure I am taking time off of work and intentionally leaning into fun. I found that fun is actually fun. Go figure!

You may be the opposite. Maybe you are "all fun" and are overwhelmed by your life-plate. Either way, we all need to make sure our life-plate has that "pop of color."

Keeping it Real:

When was the last time you had fun?

Do you regularly make time for fun?

What are your hobbies?

How often do you get to do your hobbies?

PLATING
Presentation Isn't Really Everything

My husband and I like to watch cooking competition shows. I find it comical for the contestants to have to create a gourmet meal out of strange ingredients. "You have 30 minutes to make 3 courses with the main ingredient being a rutabaga. Go!" The contestants run around and grab all these other ingredients that we all "should" have in our everyday pantries and then somehow create these fabulous meals. My favorite part is near the end of their time when they have to "plate" the food. They must ensure that the presentation is pleasing.

I have watched contestants with the most amazing looking plate have gross, undercooked food. I have also seen some where their presentation was less than satisfactory, but their flavors were spot on, and they ended up winning the competition. Our lesson from this...presentation isn't always everything.

It's time to get really real. Let me take you back again to the story in the Introduction. One of the comments that was made to me was, "You think that you are hiding it, but I can see through you...you are overwhelmed and headed for burnout." This comment really stung. Was I trying to present myself as something that I'm not? As I processed all of this, I had to admit to myself that I was trying to paint a picture that I had it all together. I can do all things…be all the things…all the time. I was lying to myself that I was struggling. I didn't want to admit it. I took the time to really search within. I found that on the outside, I was looking pretty good. I had just about everyone fooled…even myself. Inside, I was empty and undone.

My friend, this is not the life we are meant to lead. Our soul needs to be healthy. Our body needs to be healthy. Our mind needs to be healthy. The only way we get this is by leaning fully on Christ and HIS plans for our life. This includes our life-plate. Turning our life-plates over to Him. Allowing Him to guide us. Him giving us the courage to say "no" to some things. Him giving us the strength to take on things we don't think we can do. At our VBS this summer, we went through the life of Joseph, and we memorized this verse together:

"And we know [with great confidence] that God [who is deeply concerned about us] causes all things to work together [as a plan] for good for those who love God, to those who are called according to His plan and purpose."
-Romans 8:28 (AMP)

If you are finding yourself in burnout, or almost in burnout…God is concerned about you. This isn't the end. He can and will work this out for you.

He loves you.

He has called you.
He has a plan for you…still.

Keeping it Real:

Are you being real?

Are you hiding behind "good plating"?

PAPER PLATES & FINE CHINA
Who are you giving your best to?

Back in the day (I'm not as old as I sound), when you were engaged to be married you would go and create a bridal registry so that everyone could buy you the things you needed as you started your life together. One of the main things that was generally put onto the bridal registry was fine china. The bride got to go and pick out what china pattern she wanted. This was a really big deal. This choice basically defined your taste as a woman. All of your family and friends would go and purchase pieces of this fine china for you so that you would have the complete set. They would even make sure you had serving platters, serving bowls, butter dishes, and gravy boats - all the while judging your choice of the pattern, of course. Like I said, this was a big deal.

Fast forward, you are now married. You now own a china cabinet. This is a cabinet that is specifically for this fine china that was purchased for you. It was put into this cabinet with glass doors for all to admire, only to be taken out to use once, maybe twice a year…if you were lucky. It was fine china, and we only used it when someone very important came to dinner. That is when we would put our best foot forward.

The rest of the time, you would serve the meals on paper plates. Let's face it, no one wants to wash more dishes than they have to. We are going to put in as little effort as possible for the ones that we love and who mean the most to us. No, they don't qualify for the extra effort of the fine china. Paper plates will do. Oh, now sometimes we will pull out those little wicker paper plate holder things to be a little fancy, but it is still little effort. As far as serving dishes. No. Just put the pan in the middle of the table and let them scoop their food right out of the pan. Serving dishes are too much effort. We only reserve that effort for really important people that we are trying to impress and who don't even notice our effort.

Yes, I am being sarcastic, but there is so much truth in this. How many of us have found that as we look at the lists of our life-plate that we are serving up, the best of what we have goes to others, other things, other places, etc. and leaves little effort left over for the ones we love the most? I hate to confess this, but I have been guilty of this. Of course, it was not intentional. But how many times do we realize we are doing it and don't make a change? Our spouse, our kids, our family deserve the best of us…not the remnants of our efforts.

May I take this a step further? Are you serving God on fine china? Or, are you serving Him from a paper plate? How much effort are you putting in? What is getting your best effort?

When we give God our best, our first fruits, I truly believe He honors that. I have seen Him do it for me time and time again. He stretches my days, works out my schedule, and gives me wisdom.

For the record, I am not against paper plates. I have a Costco sized package of them in my house at all times. Paper plates are a wonderful invention and really help us with our life-plate responsibilities. I just want to challenge you, my friend, to really search your life-plate and see what you are serving on the fine china.

Keeping it Real:

How close to burnout do you feel right now?

What's on your fine china?

HOW

How to know if you are headed for burnout (or already there)

We have already answered the question of how to become burned out, so let's examine how you know if you are burned out or headed in that direction. There are many signs that alert you. These signs are a gift to us. We can use the signs to be self-aware and choose to change our behaviors to avoid burnout. Like I said, burnout is avoidable, IF WE WATCH FOR THE SIGNS AND CHOOSE TO CHANGE.

Here are some signs to let you know that you are headed for burnout (or are already there):

1. You have a lack of motivation for something that you used to love.
2. Your productivity is inconsistent.
3. You only do what you absolutely have to do.
4. You often find yourself overwhelmed and anxious on a daily basis.
5. You don't even know where to start on your to-do list.
6. Instead of tackling anything on your to-do list, you shut down and just take a nap.

7. You are easily irritated and frustrated with family and co-workers.
8. You find yourself cynical about your job and those around you.
9. You find it more and more difficult to keep up with basic communication (emails, texts.)
10. Your spouse is feeling neglected.
11. Your children are begging for you to spend time with them.
12. You are behind on your household duties, and seem to always stay behind on them..
13. Those that normally come to you are not coming to you because you "seem too busy" to help them like you usually would.
14. People around you start their sentences with, "I hate to bother you because I know you are so busy, but...."
15. The idea of a "Sabbath" is the furthest from your mind or something in a fairytale.
16. Your attitude, in general, becomes more and more negative.
17. You struggle with focus and concentration.
18. Your sleep habits are all over the place.
19. Your diet is unhealthy/and or inconsistent.
20. Your health, in general, is being neglected or is suffering.

If you have any of these signs, it's time to stop, do some self-assessing, and make some changes to your life-plate. Do it now before the burnout gets out of control. You may be able to make a few simple tweaks that will make all the difference.

However, leave it undone and it will lead to frustration, anxiety, and burnout.

Burnout is real and burnout is hard, however, there can be life after burnout. Unfortunately, I had to learn this the hard way. It took me more than once to figure out God does not intend for us to live a life that leads to burnout. God expects us to be healthy….body, soul, and mind. There is nothing wrong with living life with a full plate. Having a life full of awesome things can be rewarding and fulfilling. However, if your plate is full and your heart is empty, burnout is imminent.

Know that you CAN be healed from a life of burnout. God can and will heal your heart. He sees you. He loves you. He wants the best for you so you can be confident in that. The enemy will want nothing more than to make you second guess yourself and the power of God within you.

May your heart be fuller than your plate.

Keeping it Real:

How many of these signs of burnout are you exhibiting?

Are you surprised by any of the signs?

Are there any glaring changes you can make right now?

Have you experienced life after burnout or know someone who has?

DEBBIE RHOADS

If you asked Debbie how she got into Children's Ministry, she would tell you that she didn't go looking for it, Children's Ministry chose her. Debbie has been in ministry for over 30 years, 20 of those specifically dedicated to children's ministry. Throughout her time in ministry, she has served in churches of all sizes: big, small, multi-site, and mega-church. She has held the roles of not only Children's Pastor, but also as NextGen Pastor, and Leadership Development Director. Debbie is currently the Children's Ministry Director at Grace Chapel in Franklin, Tennessee.

Debbie and her husband reside in Franklin, Tennessee. Their two adult children, boys, also live in the Nashville area. Debbie loves to travel and experience new things, but her absolute favorite thing is being "Gigi" to her adorable grandson and her precious granddaughter.

www.ingramcontent.com/pod-product-compliance
Lightning Source LLC
Chambersburg PA
CBHW070443130626
46553CB00006B/2283